Craving Stardust

Illustrations and cover art by Eva Carballeira Rabuñal.

ISBN: 9780578788470

Craving Stardust

Morgan Toll

Illustrations and cover art by
Eva Carballeira Rabuñal

It is said that all humans are made
of stardust.

And what a life it's been . . . craving
all these years to be like them, only
to discover the universe within you
and what it truly means to feel alive.

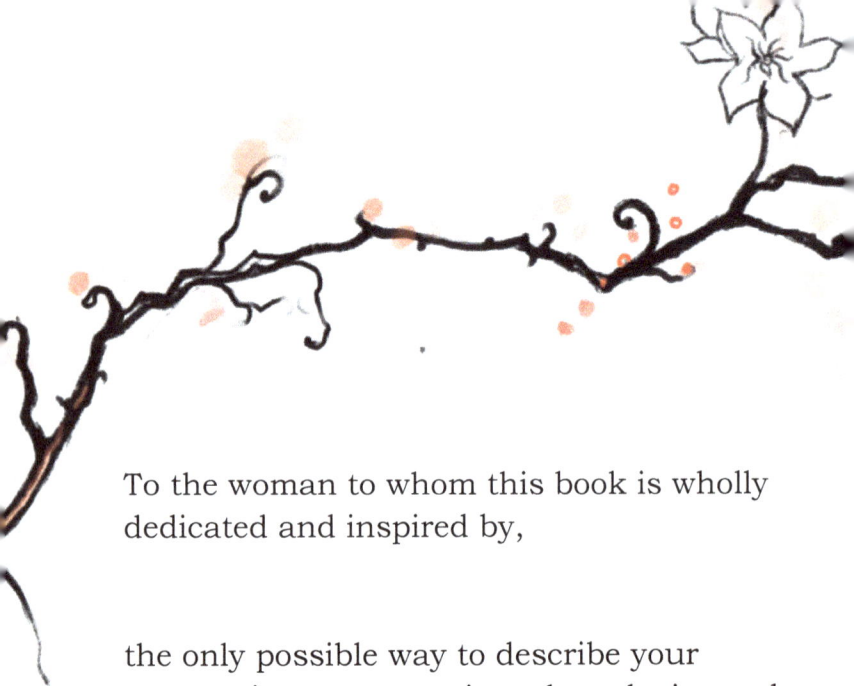

To the woman to whom this book is wholly dedicated and inspired by,

the only possible way to describe your essence is to compare it to the galaxies and the stars . . .

but even then, the universe itself isn't grand enough to hold the extent of your wonder.

So I'll spend my whole life searching . . .

searching for the words that can properly capture all of who you are.

. . . For knowing you

is all of the poetry I could ever need.

The years between us make me wonder
if on a sleepless night,
the stars that rested upon your
windowsill, illuminating your twenty-
five-year-old crystal tears, conjured
together to form a soul that was born to
search for you.

And I may find you many moons later,
reminding you of how the stars knew

even then,

of the power that was forever engraved
within your bones.

*How does one possibly gaze up
at the stars and not feel the stark
memory of your eyes shining back
at them?*

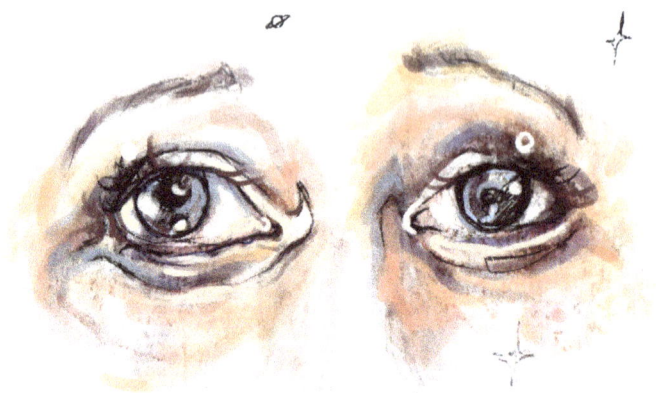

You're a rose in a field of Venus flytraps; fierce, yet delicately beautiful, and oddly placed in a world that is hungry for madness.

You may think you've hidden
yourself from the world . . .

but darling,

your smile explodes with
pieces of your soul

and if one pays attention . . .

they'll see every single molecule of your
magic . . . even in the darkest and
deepest places of your mind.

You're the mystery that no one understands,

yet everyone wants to be.

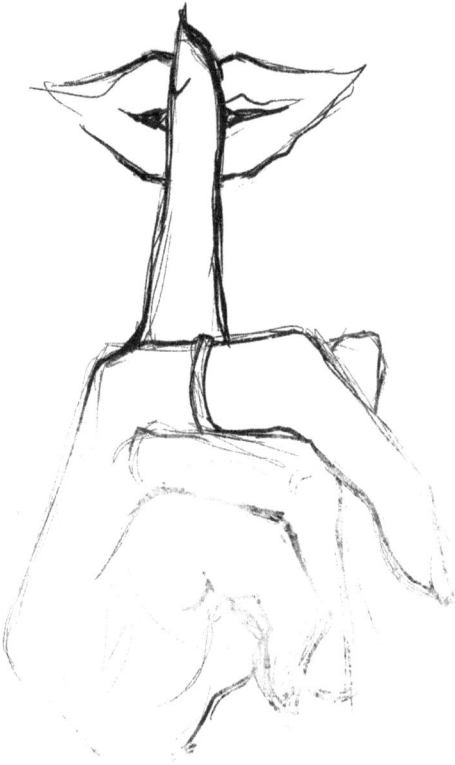

All they really are is stardust . . .

and you, a magnitude of stars,

exploding in every direction, unsure of
where you'll land.

Not knowing that every time you fall, you
become like fireworks . . .

lighting up and filling the empty gray with
every color in the sky.

So *fall* . . .

fall because there's nothing,

not an ounce, that can hold you
back . . .

that can prove that you're not
extraordinary.

I can't comprehend how anyone
could live a life without you

for even when you're near me . . .

I miss you.

You're not just a chapter in my story; you're a whole story in itself.

A whole novel . . .

A whole series . . .

One that I'll never want to finish writing.

I only ever want to write about you . . .

I want my words to be yours.

To know that I will miss every important
moment in your life feels as if I'm being
tied down in an ocean,

unable to breathe . . . knowing I will
never be able to reach the top for air.

You may never fully understand your power . . .

how with one look you can create an apocalypse,

 and with another,

realign every planet in the sky.

To know the map inside your mind was like knowing the greatest secret in the world,

and you kept it hidden . . .

sometimes, even from yourself.

You're a rare wave of infinite
magic.

For without knowing,

you ignite a fiery spell that can
burn every ounce of coldness in
my heart

and I'm dizzy . . .

lost in the smoke of your
enchantment.

I wish to memorize the melody of your voice and play it like the lyrics of a song that never gets old,

for the vibrations of your sound, even from a simple

hi

comforts me in times where only empty silence numbs the chaos in my head.

You are, without any exception,
the most beautiful and rare of all
creation

and they will never know to what
extent I see,

and I could never . . . not *ever*, say
or feel what swims like nails inside
my head,

as the thoughts would *pierce* right
through me

like the dreams so desperately
waiting to escape, but trapped by
odd circumstances and a life that
once was and will *always* be
separated.

In all the ways you are particular and contained . . .

   your heart roams with a wild intensity.

Sometimes, I can even catch a glimpse of it between the soft edges of your smile.

The thought of being caught
between the corners of your mind,

   even for just a moment,

   would be worth every
absurdity that haunted my soul.

The sound of your name burns inside of me . . .

it leaves me breathless.

Your scent rattles through my veins.

   You are fresh coffee,

   cigarette smoke,

   and a deep unfathomable desire.

It pulls me in.

Entrances me.

Consumes me.

You're beautiful in a way that is
dangerous . . .

                       that haunts and teases.

It radiates and pulls one in,

            hovering over the eyes and
begging to be touched;

lingering in one's mind so that every
wonder of the world is traced with the
outline of *you*.

I would give you all of my secrets,

just to know what you are thinking

when the tip of your glasses rests
between the center of your lips.

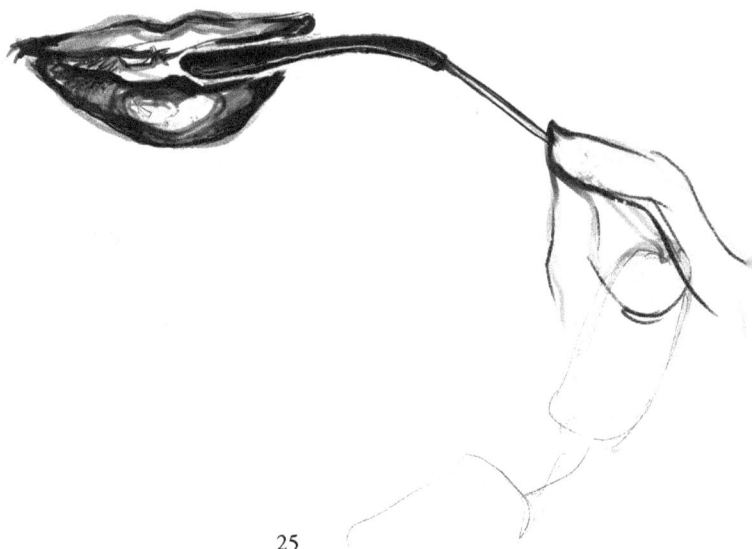

Breathe into me, breathe so deep
that I'll feel like I'm drowning.

For I need your soul in the way
that my bloodstream needs water
in order to survive.

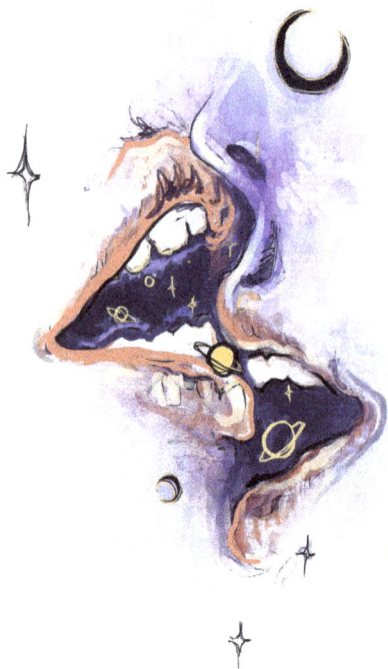

Why does this mismatched puzzle
fit so perfectly inside my realm?

My only answer could be that my
life was simply mixed-up chaos
waiting for your magic . . .

waiting my whole life to see
something so extraordinary.

No matter the clutter, stress, and absurdity the world entails

I hope you find calmness in knowing that all of the broken and missing pieces still fit together to make the amazing person that you are.

Even in the darkest days,

you still have stars in your eyes,

and they are always shining.

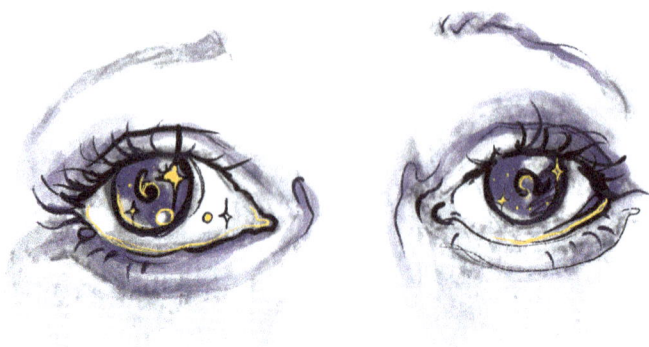

Darling,

I hope you live a life so full that the world becomes a void without you.

Time doesn't always move forward.

It moves wildly,

like a spin top on a glass table . . .

unsure of the direction it's going
and often so close to falling off the
edge.

It's as if I have given you a looking
glass and shown you pieces of my
soul in which I can't recover.

As if I had just ripped out
a part of me
and gave it to you.

The thoughts tremble and wrestle inside my head, fighting between what I know, what I wish I knew . . . and what I wish I could tell you.

For the spark between reality and the visions that grasp so tightly in my lungs becomes like glass . . .

formed inside your mysterious eyes and stained with the fingerprints of the truth you cannot hide.

I knew you weren't and could
never be mine . . .

but in that moment,

with you wrapped tightly in my
arms, with your hair draped over
my hands, and the sound of your
voice cracking as our hearts
crushed deeply and painfully
inside,

I knew in some unconventional
way . . . that we belonged to each
other . . .

so I held on just a little longer.

I'm not jealous of him because you love him, or that he fills your heart with joy.

I love everything that gives you light in this world.

I'm jealous that he's grown so used to waking up beside you that he takes those moments for granted,

that he sometimes forgets how rare and special you truly are.

For your magic is the only thing that fills my mind, and I'll never have the privilege to tire of your morning eyes.

I can't bear the thought of losing you . . .

but what might terrify me even more
is to be the reason of your pain . . .
of your disappointment.

For I have experienced the grand
pleasure of being the reason a glowing
smile sneaks upon your face . . .

and I would shatter to pieces . . .

to absolute *nothing*

if it were I who made it vanish.

My dreams are stained with the memories of you . . .

and I don't ever want to wake up.

I'll never forget the warmth in your eyes when the snow started to fall.

I stood gazing underneath it, and from under your roof you tugged me close

so that a single snowflake wouldn't touch my skin.

And for a moment,

time froze . . .

and I swore it belonged to me.

Learning to live without you

is like learning to breathe without
the lungs inside my chest.

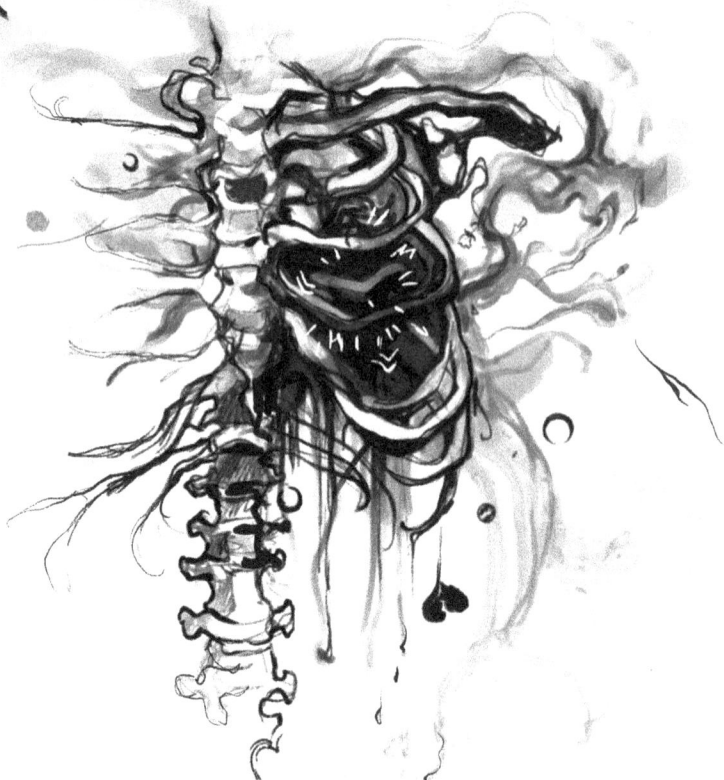

I'll spend my whole life . . . my
whole life trying to fill the empty
pieces,

the ones I never even knew
existed until you left . . .

for what a curse it is,

to have felt so impeccably full
with you beside me.

Your silence is a ribbon threaded between my ribs, suffocating my lungs.

It is a thick, cold, and sticky liquid that drowns my heart.

It is a haunting anticipation of whether there are words unspoken, or any words at all.

Lie to me.

Do whatever it takes,

whatever you need to do to keep me around.

For I can survive a life without you . . .

but how am I to live?

I know I say it over and over and
over again . . .

but it still doesn't hold as much
meaning as it should, and
sometimes they're the only words I
can find to explain how I feel.

So I'll say it again, hoping that in
some way the feeling will
transcend, absorbing into the air
so that it may somehow reach
you . . .

I miss you.

I miss every detail.

I would spend one hundred thousand years of darkness just to see your light one more time,

just to see you smile.

Life is beautiful in the way that we can see things so perfectly wonderful, even in the disaster.

For when you feel like a disaster . . .

I will always remind you that you're a hurricane of wonderful.

A stranger told me that my eyes are filled with wonder.

I smiled, secretly knowing that they are drenched with the memories of you.

Even in the end,

even when the sky rips open and
takes me from this earth . . .

the only thing that should make
sense,

*even when all of this is still mixed-
up madness . . .*

the only thing that should be
certain

is that you so drastically lit up
the world.

It is with great certainty that the earth
feels it . . .

for it's apparent in how the wind catches
your hair and how the golden honey
colored strip of sun lays across your
daisy and dandelion field lips as you smile

just as I held my breath when I first saw
your eyes, swimming and lost inside
you, and felt a feverish warning shake
within me as I knew it was an
impractical and insuppressible force.

But I would embrace it anyway

even if I were to give you every inch of my
soul with no return,

even if you were far too distant, far too
unattainable to reach,

I would allow it to course through my veins
in every moment between the seconds. In
every part of who I am until it eventually,
permanently, existed within me.

Because just like the earth that
sprinkles sunsets that warm your icy blue
eyes and sends lightning storms to remind
you of your raging power,

I knew that it was inevitable and impossible to contain

for knowing you is to accept it as an unstoppable surety.

And I do.

I feel it and I know,

for all that you are,

for every decision that you make,

for simply just existing . . .

I love you.

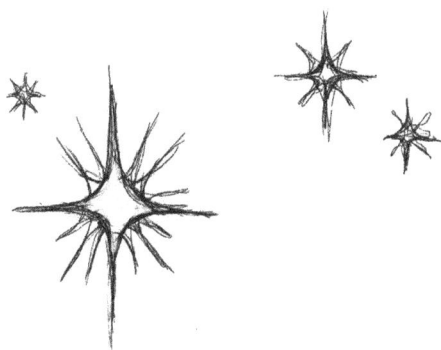

A letter to her.

I worry they may never know . . .

that these words will fail me . . .

that it won't ever be enough.

But how am I to write it all down?

Every snatched moment . . . every
memory . . .

The way your luminous eyes radiate
with sunshine when you tell a story or
talk about someone you love . . .

The way your kindness and beauty spill
out of you like the billowing smoke from
a rocket ship when you laugh . . .

The way your mind searches, curious,
and exhilaratingly sure all at the same
time.

How am I to explain the things that I have spent countless exasperating hours trying to find the answers to?

The swirling prophetic dreams that sent whispers of you before I even knew your name . . .

the endless, tenacious minutes of you dancing in my head like speckled starlight . . .

those raw, euphoric, heart-pounding moments of you walking into a room,

and the nights spent with tears soaking my pillowcase, questioning why, and how . . . and yet thanking you all at the same time.

You came out of nowhere . . .

like a shooting star, unexpected and completely magical

and I feel incredibly fortunate that you welcomed me into your realm and allowed me to have been in even the smallest part of your story.

For no matter what happens in my life, I will always, *always* look back on these glimpses of you and be reminded of that magic.

. . . But how am I to capture it?

How will the words stick to these pages so that years from now someone may read them and feel the celestial impact of *you*?

Will they even believe it?

For how is it possible to grasp this feeling . . . when these phrases are immaterial compared to the gravity of knowing you.

And I will hold on to it forever . . .

Seeing you in every word I will ever write, in every day that passes by, in every star-filled sky . . .

So that even in my dying breath, I will feel a surging gratitude, flooding with the memories of that galaxy within you.

I say it again . . .

You're a spectacle that burns the brightest fire in every person who is lucky enough to see you.

And I will spend every breath-filled moment immersed with a dire hope that somehow, in some way, your essence will be lined within the fibers of these pages so that those who read them will be captivated and ignited by the blazing fire that you are.

For knowing you has been the greatest adventure of my life, and I am passionately compelled to do everything in my power to share your light with the world.

All of this is to say, my darling . . .

that even if my words fail me, you won't ever, *ever* be forgotten.

Like all things,
being without her is both empty and full.

Empty because I wish so badly that if I
turned around I could see her there,
smiling and consumed in her own world.

Empty because the air is silent and
lonely without her laughter.

Empty because every single molecule
without her essence seems foreign and
damp.

> *Though, despite those things,*

> *it is full.*

> *Full because I knew her.*

> *Full because although she's far too*
> *distant to reach, every moment is*
> *engraved with the thoughts of*
> *knowing her. The thoughts of her*
> *energy and beauty.*

And because of that, she's not just in one
place, but in every place. Sprinkled upon
everything like magic.

And she's traveled far beyond,
surpassing what she ever thought she
could.

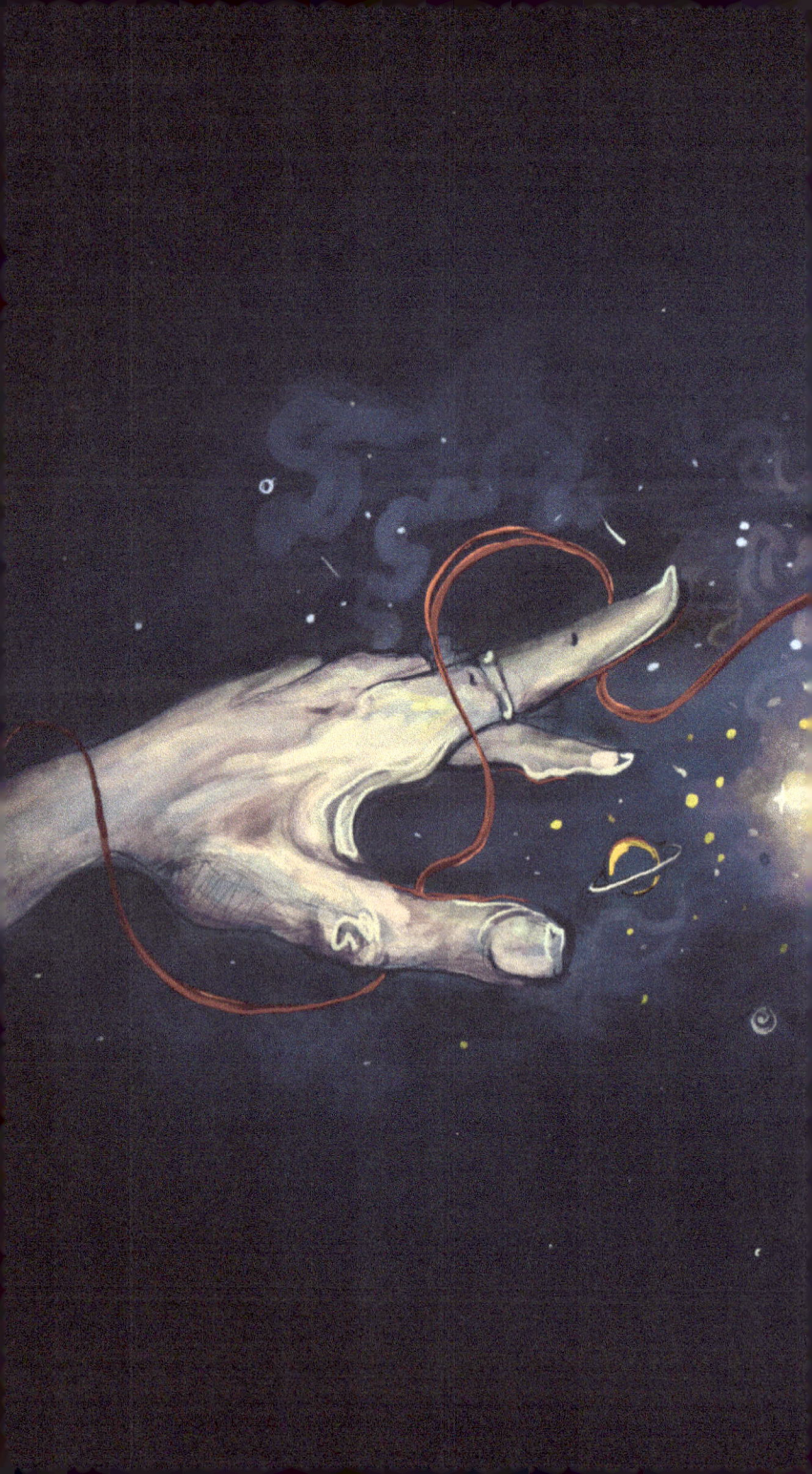

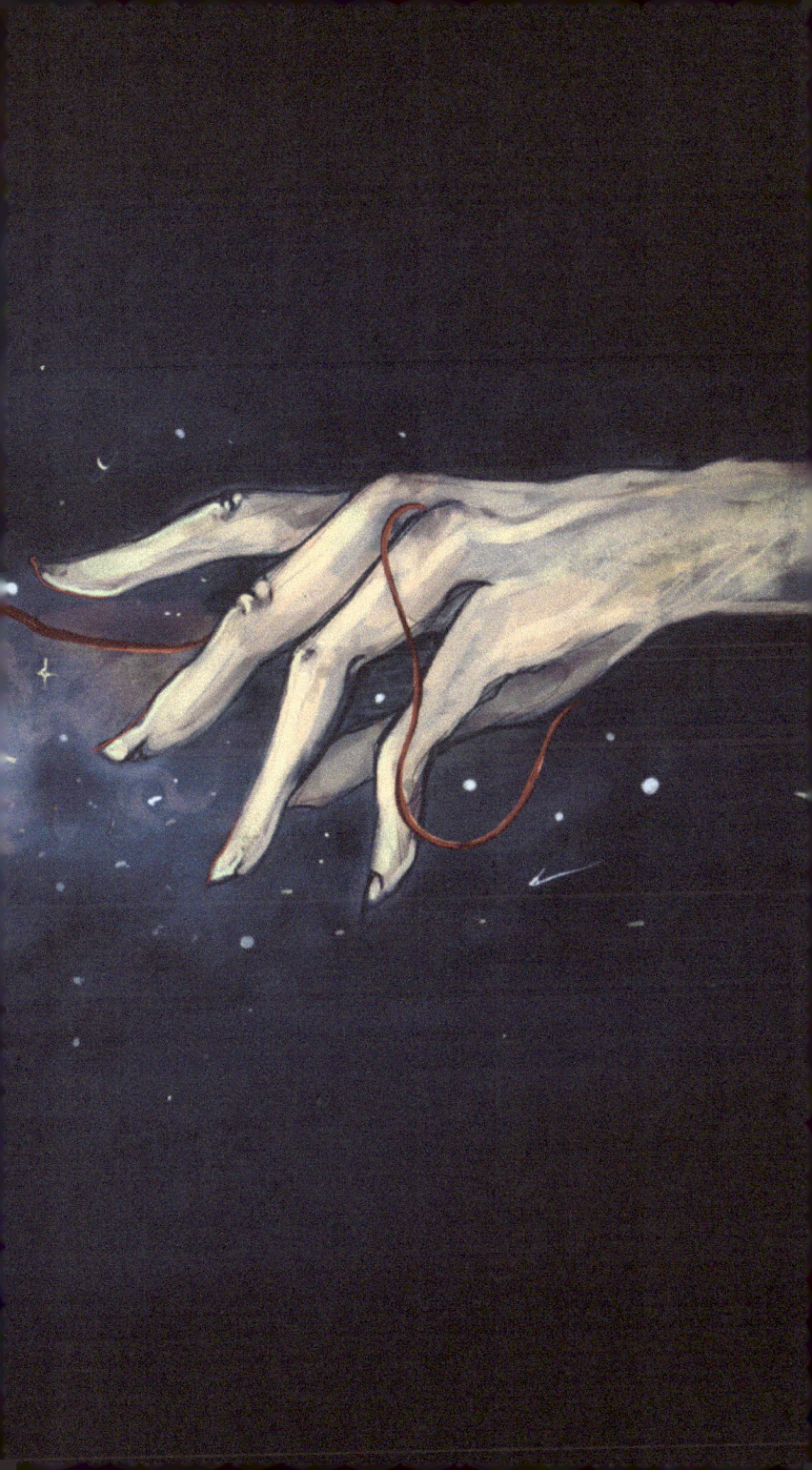

May 2, 2019

I'm standing in a room

where nothing quite makes sense

where shadows on the wall are speaking
secrets so intense.

They tell me of a woman

whose eyes are made of stars,

whose life is filled with joyful laughs that
have covered many scars.

The world has tried to break her,

they've pinned her down with chains,

but they couldn't see her truth . . .

the *lightning* in her veins.

There's something about the way she
stares,

the universe stands still.

The shooting stars could spark and
burst and fall down to her will.

Yet people seem to overlook the power of
her soul

and they laugh in all their ignorance at
the life they thought they stole.

For they could hold a million fireflies and
it could not compare

to the light that shines within her,

to the *moonbeams* in her hair.

The sweetness in her cosmic voice could
vanish all their lies

and extinguish all the demons that roam
the darkened skies.

For no one but the shadows could see her
benevolent truth

and how her empyreal essence has been
infinite since youth.

And though the world has thrown her
treasures,

to her the stars have shined . . .

it could never begin to measure

to her bold and heart-stopping mind.

For her enchanting delicate hands have
held the wind with strife

as she gave her heart to those she's
loved,

as she's sacrificed her life.

And the sparkling stardust in her smile

trapped between time and space

would linger for just a little longer to fill
that empty place.

The strength she holds is so severe it
could make the planets spin

and the magnetic pull of her bewitching
breath could pull you from within.

The shadows grab and tug me close,

they whisper of her gaze

and how the lucky ones have spent with
her their days.

For the world may sometimes crumble,

it falls and breaks and dies,

but no one could steal the galaxy . . .

the *galaxy* in her eyes.

ABOUT THE AUTHOR

"My brain hums with scraps of poetry and madness."
—Virginia Woolf

I've spent the entirety of my life escaping by creating characters from the worlds inside my head, but never did I imagine that I would find something so strikingly beautiful and rare within my own reality. This book was put together from excerpts of letters and diary entries of a time that I only hope to capture so that the memories of *her* are never lost.

- **M.**

Find us on Instagram: @cravingstardust

www.cravingstardust.com